HAMMOND

the space atlas

Mapmakers for the 21st Century

Published in the United States, Canada, and Puerto Rico
by Hammond World Atlas Corporation
Union, New Jersey 07083
www.hammondmap.com

Created and produced by Nicholas Harris, Claire Aston
and Emma Godfrey, Orpheus Books Ltd.

Text Nicholas Harris

Consultant David Hawksett, researcher in Planetary Science at
University of Lancaster, England

Illustrated by Sebastian Quigley *(Linden Artists)*

Other illustrators Gary Hincks, Inklink Firenze, Lee Montgomery,
Steve Noon, Thomas Trojer, Martin Woodward

ISBN 0-8437-1912-5

Printed and bound in Belgium.

CONTENTS

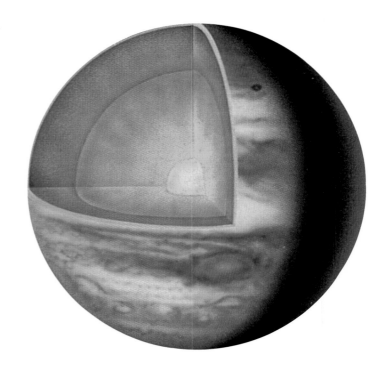

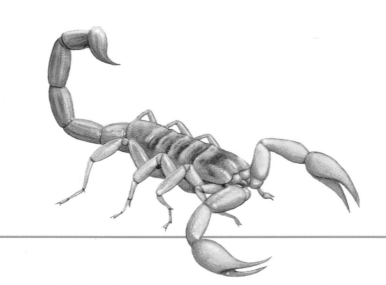

THE UNIVERSE

THE UNIVERSE consists of everything that we know to exist: stars, planets, rocks, people, and so on. It even includes empty space. Nearly all the visible matter in the Universe is contained in galaxies. About 100 billion galaxies are grouped into giant clouds, called super-clusters, spread out like a net *(above)*.

The Universe probably began in a huge explosion about 13.7 billion years ago. All matter, energy—even time itself—were created during this "Big Bang." The Universe inflated like a balloon *(below)*, with galaxies moving away from one another.

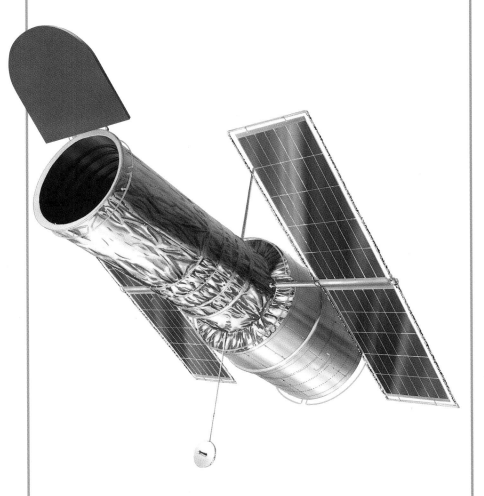

STARS AND GALAXIES

STARS are giant spinning balls of hot gases. They vary enormously in size (Betelgeuse in the constellation of Orion is 800 times the size of the Sun), and by the amount of light they give off.

Galaxies are vast collections of stars. The Solar System is located in the Milky Way Galaxy *(right)*. It has a bulge in the center (the nucleus) and four arms spiraling out from it. The nucleus is a mass of old red and yellow stars. New stars form in the arms.

Crux-Centaurus Arm

Perseus Arm

Nucleus

Orion Arm

Sun

A star is born when a cloud of dust and gas in space, known as a nebula, compresses under the force of gravity to become a dense blob, called a protostar (1). It becomes so hot that it starts to produce its own energy in its core. Soon, gas and dust are blown away (2). Sometimes, a spinning disk of gas and dust results, which may eventually become the birthplace of new planets (3).

The star now spends the next few billion years of its life as a main sequence star, like our Sun (4). But when the fuel it uses to produce energy runs out, the star swells into a red giant (5). Most stars become red giants, but some much heavier ones become supergiants (6). Eventually, a supergiant blasts apart in a mighty explosion called a supernova (7). It ends its days as a neutron star or a black hole (8).

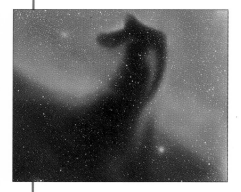

The Horsehead Nebula is a giant cloud of dust and gas, a birthplace of stars.

Milky Way Galaxy

Sagittarius Arm

The Crab Nebula *(left)* is all that remains of a supernova, the gigantic explosion of a supergiant star. It consists of dust and gas slowly drifting off into space. The supernova that created it took place in 1054 and was witnessed and recorded by Chinese astronomers.

A red giant does not explode. Instead, its outer layers flake away into space leaving a planetary nebula *(right)* with a white dwarf at its core.

After a supernova, the old star's core may be so dense that it collapses in on itself. The core may shrink to a tiny point, surrounded by a region of space where gravity is so strong that nothing, not even light, can escape from it. Scientists call these places black holes. They are invisible, but it is possible to find them by studying their effects on other objects. This massive blue star *(below),* for example, is being dragged around in a circle before being sucked in by a black hole.

Galaxies are not normally found on their own. Most are clumped together in clusters. Our own galaxy, the Milky Way, belongs to a cluster called the Local Group. The Local Group contains different types of galaxies: spirals (like the Milky Way), barred spirals (a little different from the spirals' catherine wheel shape), ellipticals (shaped like ovals), and irregulars (no obvious shape).

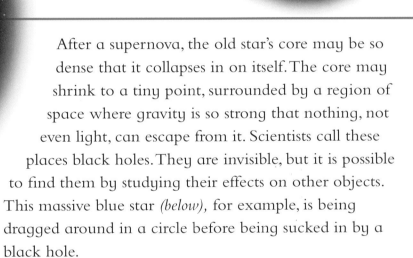

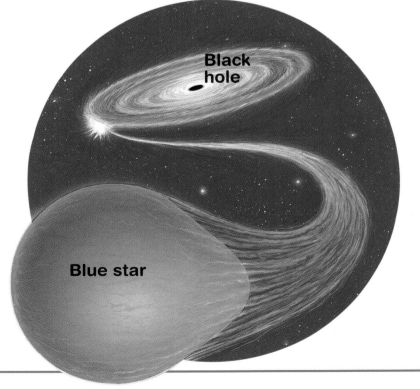

Black hole

Blue star

THE SUN

THE SUN is a star, just one of billions of stars in the Milky Way Galaxy. Although nearly 1,400,000 Earths could fit inside it, it is below average size for a star.

The Sun consists almost entirely of hydrogen and helium. At its center is the core, a region where the pressure is 200 billion times what it is on Earth's surface. Here temperatures are about 25 million°F, hot enough for hydrogen to turn into helium. This chemical reaction produces massive amounts of energy, which keeps the Sun shining. The energy flows out from the core through the radiative zone to the convective zone. Here, hot gas bubbles to the surface before sinking back down to be reheated.

Arch

Flare

Moon

Corona

By coincidence, the Sun and Moon appear to be exactly the same size in the sky. When the two line up in an eclipse of the Sun, the Moon covers it almost exactly. The sky darkens and the Sun's milky-white atmosphere, the corona, becomes visible. Eclipses last a maximum of 7 minutes 31 seconds.

The surface of the Sun is called the photosphere. The temperature here is "only" 9,900°F—much cooler than at the core. Hot gas bubbles and spits like water boiling in a pan.

Flare

Because its orbit is slightly tilted, the Moon usually passes above or below the Sun as seen from Earth. Occasionally, the Moon passes directly between the Sun and Earth, causing its shadow to fall on our planet, an event known as an eclipse. Partial eclipses, when only part of the Sun is covered over, are visible over a wide area. Total eclipses, when the Sun is completely hidden, can be seen from only a narrow region.

Sun

Moon

3

2

1

Earth

1   2   3

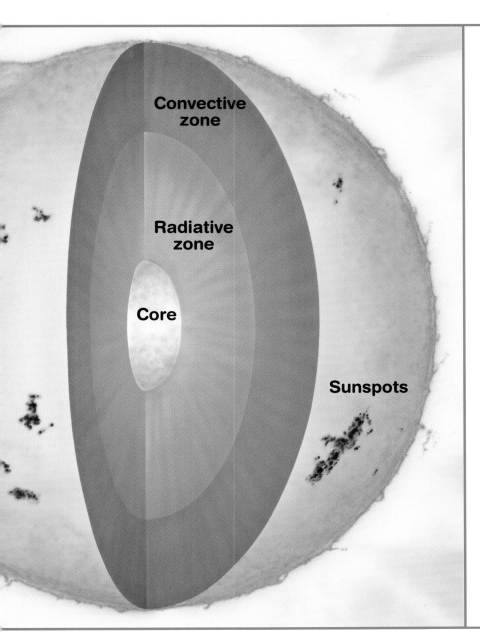

Convective zone

Radiative zone

Core

Sunspots

In about seven billion years' time, the Sun's fuel of hydrogen will start to run out. The Sun will balloon in size, becoming a red giant. The tiny disk on the left *(above)* represents the Sun as it is today. The disk on the right shows it as a red giant, one hundred times larger. Eventually the gigantic Sun will engulf the closest planets, Mercury and Venus. This *(below)* is what will happen to Earth's landscape at the same time. Its oceans and atmosphere will disappear, and its rocky surface will melt in temperatures of 2,700°F.

Prominence

Spicules

Sunspots

Flaming gas jets, called spicules, leap up. From time to time, huge arches (prominences) or tongues (flares) burst out from the surface. Dark, cooler blotches called sunspots appear where lines of magnetic force break through.

SUN DATAFILE

Diameter: 870,000 miles
Density (water=1): 1.4
Mass (Earth=1): 330,000
Rotation period at equator: 25.4 days
Rotation period at poles: 34 days
Average distance from Earth:
93 million miles
Surface temperature: 9,900°F
Composition: hydrogen (74.4%);
helium (24.9%)

The Sun compared in size to a young blue star and a red giant.

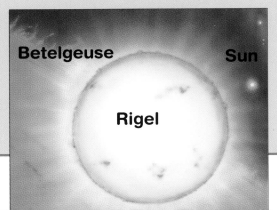

Betelgeuse   **Sun**

Rigel

THE SOLAR SYSTEM

T HE SUN lies at the center of an array of objects of different sizes, all traveling around it. Together, they are known as the Solar System. It includes the Sun itself, the nine planets, their 127 known moons, asteroids, comets, meteoroids, and vast amounts of gas and dust. It is the Sun's massive size, compared to the rest of its family, and its huge force of gravity, that keeps all these objects in orbit around it.

The planets orbit the Sun in the same counter-clockwise direction, all following an elliptical (oval), rather than circular, path. Pluto's orbit is the most elliptical. For part of its journey it lies actually inside Neptune's orbit. For the rest, it is far beyond Neptune.

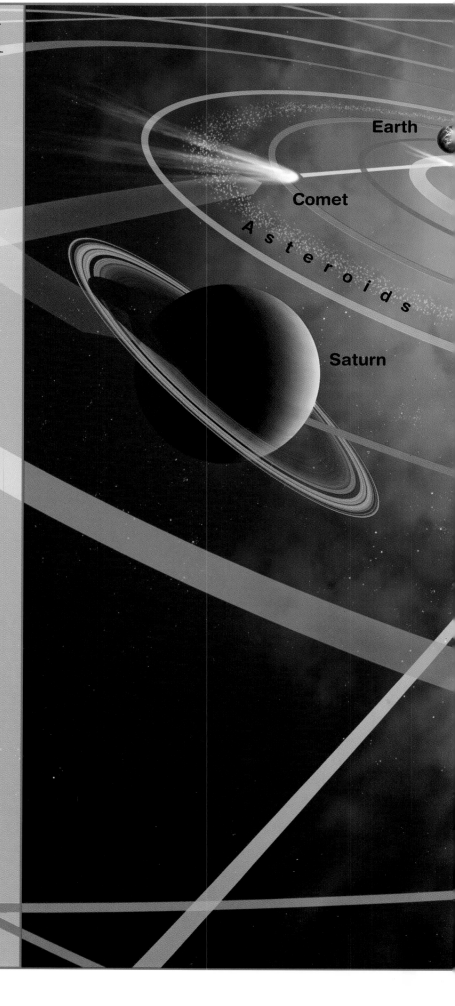

Earth

Comet

Asteroids

Saturn

Neptune

Mercury
Venus
Earth
Mars

Asteroids   Jupiter   Saturn   Uranus

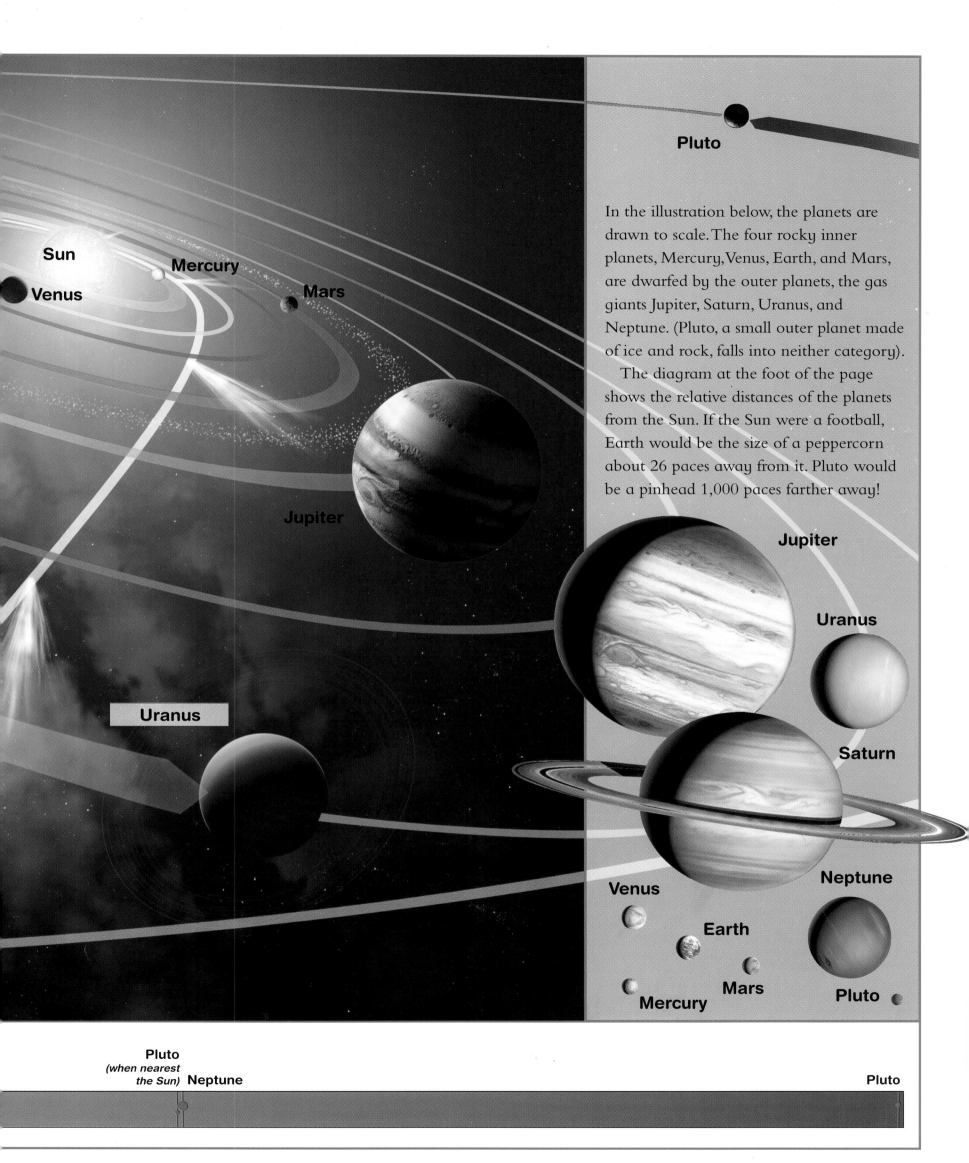

Pluto

In the illustration below, the planets are drawn to scale. The four rocky inner planets, Mercury, Venus, Earth, and Mars, are dwarfed by the outer planets, the gas giants Jupiter, Saturn, Uranus, and Neptune. (Pluto, a small outer planet made of ice and rock, falls into neither category).

The diagram at the foot of the page shows the relative distances of the planets from the Sun. If the Sun were a football, Earth would be the size of a peppercorn about 26 paces away from it. Pluto would be a pinhead 1,000 paces farther away!

Sun

Mercury

Venus

Mars

Jupiter

Uranus

Jupiter

Uranus

Saturn

Neptune

Venus

Earth

Mars

Mercury

Pluto

Pluto
(when nearest the Sun) **Neptune**

Pluto

MERCURY

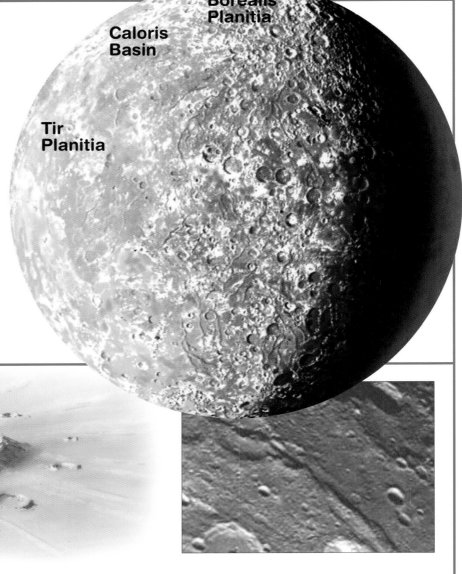

Caloris Basin

Borealis Planitia

Tir Planitia

MERCURY is the second smallest planet in the Solar System, and the closest to the Sun. It is difficult to spot from Earth: it is low on the horizon in the dawn or twilight sky.

It is always either baking or freezing on Mercury. Daytime temperatures exceed 800°F, but at night it drops to –274°F.

For the first billion or so years of its existence, Mercury was pummelled by meteorites, boulders from space crashing to its surface *(right)*. These punched saucer-shaped craters all over Mercury's surface. Whenever a crater was formed, debris was blasted out in all directions, creating smaller craters and long streaks in the ground *(above)*. Due to the absence of weather, these features have remained undisturbed ever since. In some dark craters out of the Sun's heat, water ice may possibly exist.

After the bombardment by meteorites began to ease off, Mercury's surface began to shrink, resulting in wrinkles. These appear as high cliffs on the rocky terrain. This photo of one *(above)* was taken by space probe Mariner 10 in 1974.

Mercury is the densest of all the planets apart from Earth. It has a huge metal core made of iron and nickel, surrounded by a rocky shell. Because there is almost no atmosphere on Mercury, all the heat it receives from the Sun by day disappears at night. It is also the reason why Mercury's skies remain black, even during the day.

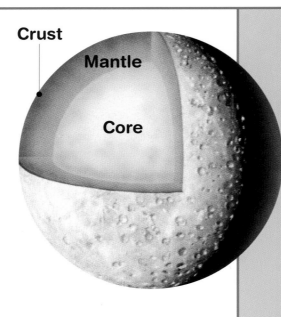

Crust

Mantle

Core

MERCURY DATAFILE

Diameter: 3,031 miles

Average density (water=1): 5.4

Surface gravity (Earth=1): 0.38

Mass (Earth=1): 0.055

Day: 58.6 Earth days

Year: 88 Earth days

Speed in orbit: 29.8 miles/sec

Average distance from the Sun: 36 million miles

Surface temperature: -274 to +806°F

Atmosphere: traces of helium

Number of moons: none

VENUS

VENUS is the most inhospitable of the inner planets. It has a constant surface temperature hotter than the melting point of lead. The air pressure is about 90 times that on Earth. The thick clouds that surround it are made of deadly sulfuric acid, and the atmosphere is made of unbreathable carbon dioxide.

Ishtar Terra

Sedna Planitia

Guinevere Planitia

Alpha Regio

Lada Terra

Venus is always surrounded by clouds *(left)*.

This is a view of Venus's rocky surface beneath its dense cloud cover *(above)*.

Beneath the clouds, Venus's surface features thousands of volcanoes surrounded by lava plains. Lava flows have cut channels that look like the work of rivers.

Venus has an internal structure similar to that of Earth, although its core is much larger. Its cloud cover, 16 miles thick, prevents most sunlight from reaching the surface. But infrared radiation from the Sun does get through. Venus's dense carbon dioxide atmosphere stops it escaping. This results in constant, extreme heat.

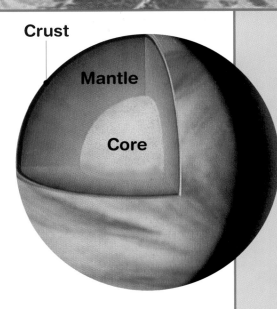

Crust

Mantle

Core

VENUS DATAFILE

Diameter: 7,525 miles

Density (water=1): 5.2

Surface gravity (Earth=1): 0.9

Mass (Earth=1) 0.81

Day: 243 Earth days

Year: 225 Earth days

Speed in orbit: 22 miles/sec

Average distance from the Sun: 67 million miles

Surface temperature: 914°F

Atmosphere: carbon dioxide, traces of nitrogen

Number of moons: none

EARTH

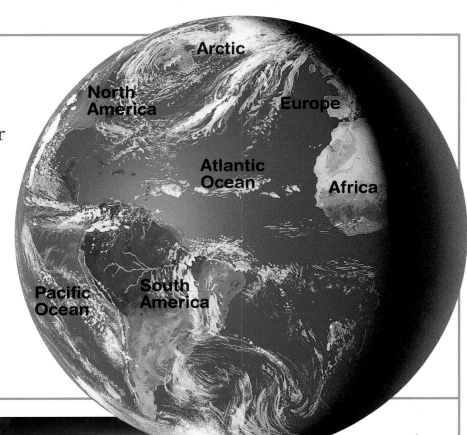

E ARTH is the only world in the Solar System which has liquid water on its surface, essential for life to exist. Earth's distance from the Sun produces exactly the right temperature range. Its atmosphere traps enough warmth to avoid extremes. It also acts as a shield against meteorite bombardment.

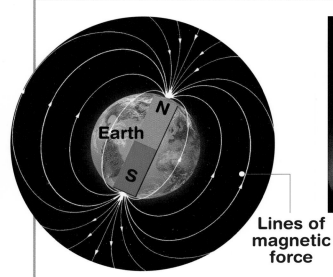

Lines of magnetic force

Earth has a magnetic field. It is strongest at the North and South Magnetic Poles. Invisible lines of force run from one pole to the other, as if Earth were a bar magnet.

Earth's magnetic field stretches out into space, producing a giant teardrop shape called the magnetosphere *(right)*. This protects us from high-energy particles that constantly stream out from the Sun, known as the solar wind.

Some of the Sun's high-energy particles *(see below left)* get through the magnetosphere near the poles. They produce patterns of glowing light in the sky called aurorae *(left)*.

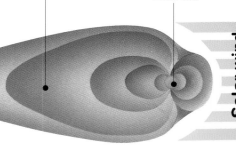

Magnetosphere

Earth

Solar wind

At the center of Earth is a ball of solid iron with a small amount of nickel. The temperature is around 13,500°F. The outer core is liquid iron. This is surrounded by a thick mantle, consisting of rock that is partly solid, partly molten. The outermost layer is a thin, rocky shell called the crust, which is fractured into large plates.

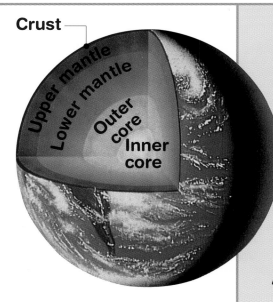

Crust

Upper mantle

Lower mantle

Outer core

Inner core

E A R T H   D A T A F I L E

Diameter: 7,926 miles

Density (water=1): 5.5

Day: 23 hours 56 minutes

Year: 365.26 days

Speed in orbit: 18.5 miles/sec

Average distance from the Sun: 93 million miles

Surface temperature: -94 to +131°F

Atmosphere: nitrogen, oxygen, argon, and water vapor

Number of moons: 1

MOON

THE MOON is a ball of rock that orbits Earth. It is a barren world, pitted with craters blasted out by meteorites billions of years ago.

The Moon may have been formed when another planet crashed into the young Earth. Rocky fragments from the impact came together to form the Moon.

Mare Frigoris
Dark
Plato crater
Mare Imbrium
Mare Serenitatis
Mare Crisium
Oceanus Procellarum
Copernicus crater
Mare Tranquillitatis

There is neither air nor liquid water on the lunar surface. (Some water ice may be found there.) Instead, it is a completely barren landscape made up of craters, mountain ranges, and wide lava plains that observers once took to be seas (and are still called by the Latin name for sea, *mare*).

The shape of the Moon seems to change from one night to the next. This is because it spins only once as it orbits Earth, so the same face points towards us at all times. When that face is turned away from the Sun, it is invisible: a New Moon (1). When it is turned towards the Sun we see a complete disk: a Full Moon (5). In between, it passes through crescent (2, 8), quarter (3, 7), and gibbous (4, 6) phases.

Earth

Sun's rays

Moon

The Moon's internal structure is not unlike Earth's. Its crust is thicker, although there are far fewer rock types than on Earth. The Moon has no atmosphere, so debris scattered by meteorite impacts billions of years ago has lain undisturbed ever since. The lack of air is responsible for a wide daily temperature range.

Crust

Mantle

Outer core

Inner core

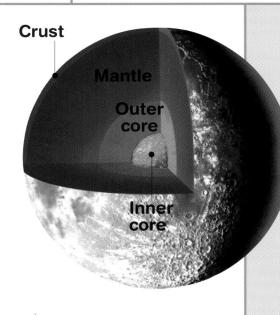

MOON DATAFILE

Diameter: 2,160 miles

Density (water=1): 3.34

Surface gravity (Earth=1): 0.16

Mass (Earth=1): 0.012

Day: 27.3 Earth days

Speed in orbit: 0.634 miles/sec

Average distance from Earth: 238,600 miles

Surface temperature: -247 to +221°F

Atmosphere: none

MARS

Tempe
Terra

Olympus Mons

Xanth
Terra

Tharsis Ridge

Valles Marineris

Aonia
Terra

MARS is the fourth planet from the Sun. It is known as the Red Planet because of the reddish color of the dust that covers it, although sometimes dark areas of rock show up when storms blow away the dust.

Dry river beds and old seashores prove that water once flowed on Mars. The only water on the surface nowadays is frozen at the poles. Frozen water also exists under the ground elsewhere. If Mars once had liquid water, it is possible that life could have existed there ...

This photo of the barren Martian surface was taken by the imager on board the Pathfinder space probe in 1997. Sojourner, a small rover vehicle, is seen near a rock scientists nicknamed "Yogi."

Mars has many volcanoes, all of which are now believed to be extinct. The most spectacular ones are found on the Tharsis Ridge, a bulge on the Martian surface. All the Tharsis volcanoes are much higher and broader than any found on Earth. Located on the edge of the Ridge, Olympus Mons towers 17 miles above the surrounding land. It is more than three times as high as 29,000-foot-high Mount Everest, the highest mountain on Earth.

The caldera (crater) at its summit measures about 50 miles across. The volcano's base spans about 400 miles. Olympus Mons is the highest mountain in the Solar System.

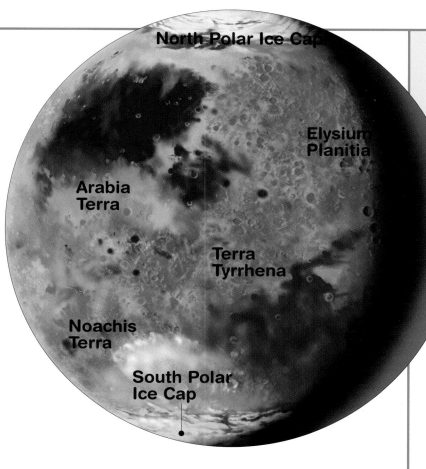

North Polar Ice Cap

Elysium
Planitia

Arabia
Terra

Terra
Tyrrhena

Noachis
Terra

South Polar
Ice Cap

MARS DATAFILE

Diameter: 4,222 miles

Average density (water=1): 3.9

Surface gravity (Earth=1): 0.4

Mass (Earth=1): 0.11

Day: 24.6 Earth hours

Year: 687 Earth days

Speed in orbit: 15 miles/sec

Average distance from the Sun: 142 million miles

Surface temperature: -184 to +77°F

Atmosphere: carbon dioxide, nitrogen

Number of moons: 2

The walls of this valley in Gorgonum Chaos region of Mars are lined with many gullies (small channels). Scientists think they may have been formed by water seeping from the ground.

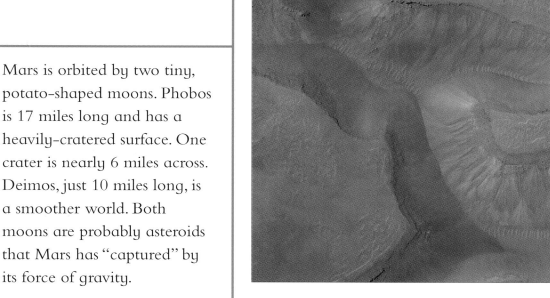

Phobos

Deimos

Mars is orbited by two tiny, potato-shaped moons. Phobos is 17 miles long and has a heavily-cratered surface. One crater is nearly 6 miles across. Deimos, just 10 miles long, is a smoother world. Both moons are probably asteroids that Mars has "captured" by its force of gravity.

The gullies (deep channels) that cover Olympus Mons' slopes, were carved out by lava flows. Skirting the base is a 3-mile-high cliff, over which lava once splashed.

Mars has a lower density than Earth, and it has no magnetic field. This means that the Red Planet probably has only quite a small, solid iron core. Between the core and the crust is a solid rocky mantle. Mars has a very thin atmosphere consisting mostly of carbon dioxide. Occasionally, there are mists of water vapor.

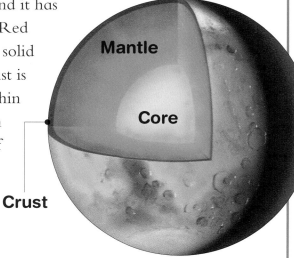

Mantle

Core

Crust

ASTEROIDS

THOUSANDS of small, irregular shaped objects, called asteroids, orbit the Sun between Mars and Jupiter. More than 4,000 have been discovered and named. The largest, Ceres, measures only about 600 miles across.

There may be up to a million asteroids measuring up to a mile or more across. Many are tiny specks, too small to be identified.

Many asteroids are heavily-cratered objects. They probably formed when early planets smashed into one another, leaving a belt of fragments. Most asteroids are rocky, which means that some of them must have come from the upper layers of a planet (Earth's upper layers are also rocky). But a few are made of metal: They must have come from the cores of old planets. Asteroids still collide with one another, producing smaller fragments of rock called meteoroids. These sometimes crash to Earth as meteorites.

Meteorites range in size from minute fragments to boulders measuring many feet across. It is feared that a large meteorite or even a complete asteroid may one day crash into Earth, punching an enormous crater in its surface. The explosion would also fill the atmosphere with dust, blotting out the sun, and lowering temperatures worldwide for years on end. No wonder that astronomers keep a careful eye on asteroids that may get too close for comfort ...

A large asteroid may have been responsible for one of the most devastating events on Earth. Some scientists believe an asteroid may have crashed into Earth 65 million years ago. The change in climate that followed wiped out the dinosaurs and many other prehistoric species.

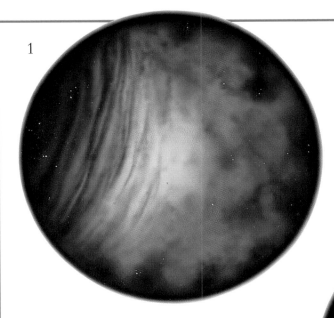

1

1 A shock wave, possibly from a star exploding nearby, causes a cloud of dust and gas to compress.

2 The cloud of dust and gas becomes a swirling disk. The center becomes hotter and denser, and begins to bulge ...

2

3 Dust clumps together to form boulders, then eventually large bodies called planetesimals.

3

ORIGIN OF THE PLANETS

BY STUDYING meteorites, scientists have been able to work out the age of the Solar System itself: 4.6 billion years. At that time, a cloud of dust and gas drifted through space. The cloud became a swirling disk of matter, with a center that became hotter and denser, eventually becoming the Sun. Particles of remaining dust clumped together and became boulders. These built up like snowballs into large balls of rock, finally becoming planets.

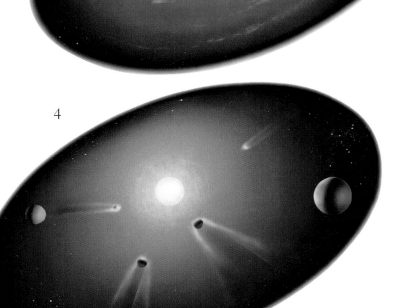

4

5

5 The Solar System today. The outer planets have held on to their atmospheres and become the gas giants. Earth and Venus develop new atmospheres.

4 A hot ball of gas—a star—forms at the center. The atmospheres of the inner planets are stripped away.

JUPITER

JUPITER is the largest of all the planets. It is big enough to contain all the other planets put together. Known as a "gas giant," because of its thick gassy outer layer, Jupiter has many moons and some faint rings made of dark grains of dust.

The colorful bands of red, white, brown, and yellow on its surface are actually clouds in Jupiter's swirling, stormy atmosphere. The planet's very quick rotation is probably responsible for separating the clouds into different color "zones" (the lighter bands) and "belts" (the darker bands). The spin also causes Jupiter to bulge at its equator.

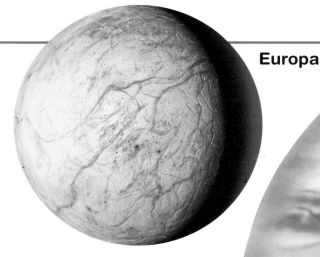

Europa

Jupiter's fourth largest moon, Europa, measures 1,950 miles across. It is a world of great interest to astronomers. Its smooth, icy surface is covered by a maze of lines. The ice sheets may be continually melting and resolidifying. Below the ice there may be a warm-water ocean. Could it be that there are living things swimming in this ocean?

Ganymede

Jupiter's four largest moons are called the Galileans, after their discoverer, Galileo. Bigger than both Mercury and Pluto, Ganymede, at 3,274 miles across, is the largest moon in the Solar System. Ganymede has an icy surface with dark, cratered plains and areas showing strange "grooved" patterns, as if someone has clawed away at its surface with a giant fork.

Callisto is Jupiter's second largest moon. It measures 2,986 miles across. For its size, it has more craters than any other planet or moon in the Solar System. Its largest crater, called Valhalla, is 370 miles in diameter, and is surrounded by a series of ripples stretching out in all directions for a distance of 1,900 miles. Callisto has a thick crust made of a mixture of water ice and rock, making it look a little like a "dirty snowball."

Callisto

Io

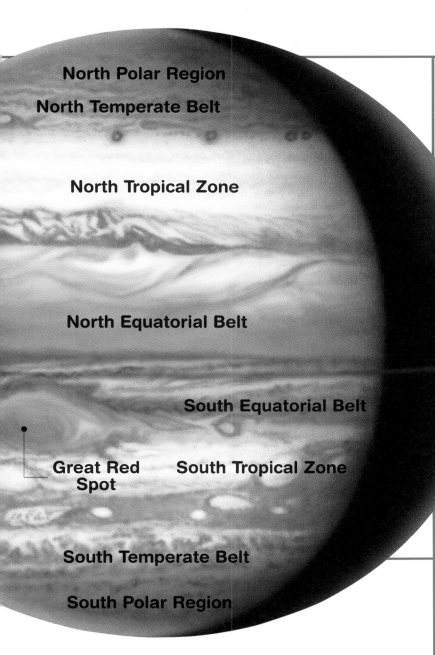

North Polar Region

North Temperate Belt

North Tropical Zone

North Equatorial Belt

South Equatorial Belt

Great Red Spot   **South Tropical Zone**

South Temperate Belt

South Polar Region

JUPITER DATAFILE

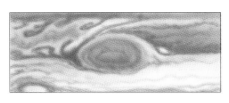

Diameter: 88,788 miles

Average density (water=1): 1.3

Surface gravity (Earth=1): 2.64

Mass (Earth=1): 318

Day: 9.8 Earth hours

Year: 11.8 Earth years

Speed in orbit: 8 miles/sec

Average distance from the Sun: 484 million miles

Surface temperature: -238°F

Atmosphere: hydrogen, helium

Number of moons: 60

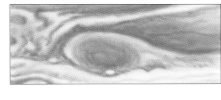

Jupiter's third largest moon, Io, is covered with active volcanoes and pools of molten rock. The volcanoes are almost continually erupting dust and sulfur dioxide gas, which bursts through from Io's rocky interior and jets some 200 miles upward into space. Io measures 2,260 miles across.

Large enough to contain at least two Earths, the Great Red Spot is actually a giant storm that has been raging for at least 300 years. Its topmost clouds rotate in a counterclockwise direction, taking about six days to make a complete turn. This sequence shows smaller storms (the white ovals) and other air currents flowing past the Spot.

The Spot is not always red. Sometimes it takes on a gray or white appearance. The red color comes from the chemical element phosphorus. It shows when material from deep below the Spot spirals upward and is exposed to sunlight.

Jupiter is mostly made of hydrogen, but only a small part of it is found in its gaseous form. Surrounding its small rocky core (actually twice the size of Earth) is a thick layer of hydrogen that is so dense it is like a metal. Above that is a layer of liquid hydrogen, then a thick atmosphere of gaseous hydrogen and helium. Its clouds are made of ammonia, methane, and water ice.

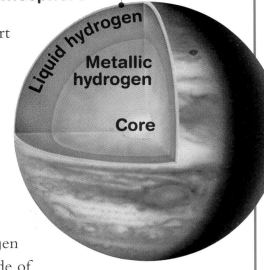

Atmosphere

Liquid hydrogen

Metallic hydrogen

Core

SATURN

S|ATURN is the second largest planet. All four gas giants have ring systems, but whereas those of Jupiter, Uranus, and Neptune are faint and narrow, Saturn's are bright and wide. The rings reach out 153,000 miles across space, a distance almost equal to that between Earth and Moon, or five times the radius of Saturn.

Like Jupiter, Saturn has a large number of moons (31 at latest count), although many are small, irregular-shaped bodies. Some even share the same orbits.

Beneath the honey-coloured haze surrounding Saturn's globe, there are layers of clouds. Strong winds and storms some-times create ripples and spots on its surface. Saturn rotates very quickly, producing a distinct bulge around its middle.

Cassini Division

Tethys

Mimas

Titan is the second largest moon in the Solar System and the only one known to have a thick atmosphere. It consists largely of nitrogen. The orange haze surrounding the moon may conceal a mountainous landscape, or a sea of methane, possibly with floating icebergs. The space probe Huygens will find out more when it arrives on Titan in late 2004.

Other Saturnian moons are cratered worlds. The Herschel crater on Mimas is a third the size of the moon itself. Icy Enceladus has a relatively smooth surface *(right)*. It may be constantly recoated by eruptions of water ice bursting through cracks in its crust.

Titan

The space probe Voyager 2 *(see page 28)* took detailed photographs of Saturn's rings. They showed that the rings were made up of billions of blocks of ice and rock. They range in size from tiny fragments the size of snowflakes, to large chunks the size of houses.

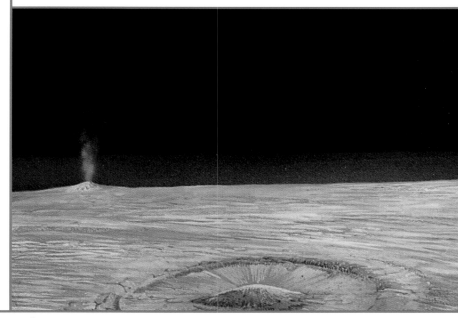

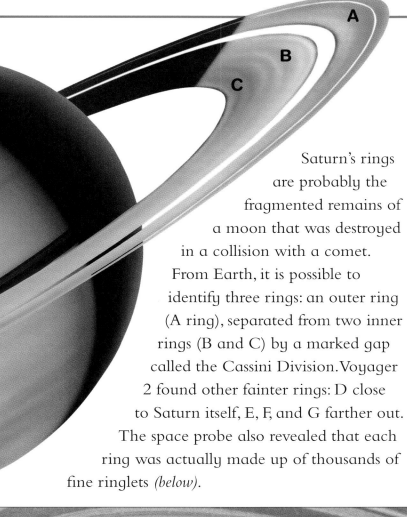

Saturn's rings are probably the fragmented remains of a moon that was destroyed in a collision with a comet. From Earth, it is possible to identify three rings: an outer ring (A ring), separated from two inner rings (B and C) by a marked gap called the Cassini Division. Voyager 2 found other fainter rings: D close to Saturn itself, E, F, and G farther out. The space probe also revealed that each ring was actually made up of thousands of fine ringlets *(below)*.

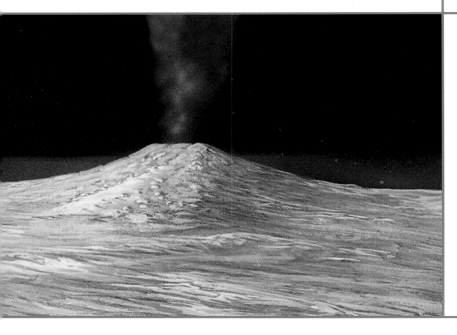

SATURN DATAFILE

Diameter: 74,901 miles

Density (water=1): 0.7

Surface gravity (Earth=1): 1.16

Mass (Earth=1) 95.2

Day: 10.2 Earth hours

Year: 29.5 Earth years

Speed in orbit: 6 miles/sec

Average distance from the Sun: 887 million miles

Surface temperature: -292°F

Atmosphere: hydrogen, helium

Number of moons: 31

Saturn's spinning axis tilts from the vertical by 26.7°. This means that our view of its rings from Earth changes as it orbits the Sun, a journey that takes 29.5 years to complete. At stages 1 and 7 on the diagram below, they are pictured edge-on and invisible to an observer on Earth. At stages 4 and 10, they are visible to us at their widest angles. Saturn's magnificent rings are easily visible from Earth through good binoculars or a small telescope.

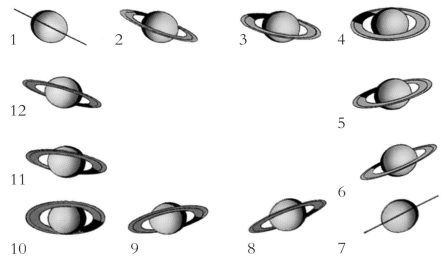

Saturn's internal structure is very similar to that of Jupiter. Its rocky core is surrounded by layers of hydrogen in metallic, liquid, and gaseous states. Its thick atmosphere contains mostly hydrogen, plus a little helium. Saturn is the least dense of all the planets. If an ocean large enough could be found, it would float!

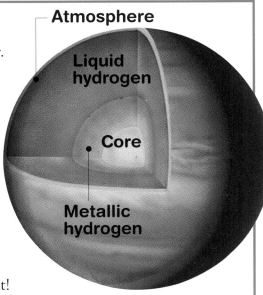

URANUS

URANUS was discovered in 1781 by German astronomer William Herschel. It was the first planet to be discovered using a telescope. We now know that Uranus is tilted at 98°, meaning that it orbits the Sun almost on its side. Each pole has some 42 years of continuous daylight, followed by 42 years of darkness.

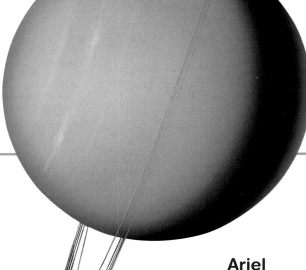

Circling Uranus's equator are 11 faint, narrow rings, made of pitch-black blocks of ice.

Ariel

Ariel, the brightest of Uranus's major moons, is crisscrossed by several grooves, some up to 12 miles deep. There are few craters, however. Recent volcanic eruptions may have covered them with smooth rock.

Measuring just 290 miles across, Miranda, one of Uranus's moons, has a very jumbled-up surface made up of grooves, canyons, and craters, including a boomerang-shaped feature. It may once have been a smooth world (1) before being blasted apart by a comet (2). Gravity held the fragments together (3), which were eventually reassembled in a haphazard fashion (4).

Uranus has a small rocky core surrounded by a mantle of water, ice, methane, and ammonia. Its thick atmosphere consists mostly of hydrogen, with some helium and methane. The surface of its globe is almost entirely featureless, apart from a few white, streaky clouds whizzing around Uranus at more than 600 miles/h.

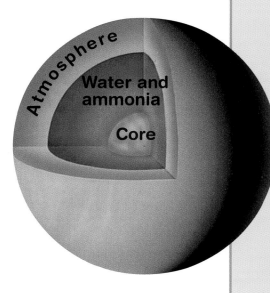

Atmosphere

Water and ammonia

Core

URANUS DATAFILE

Diameter: 31,765 miles

Density (water=1): 1.3

Surface gravity (Earth=1): 1.17

Mass (Earth=1) 14.5

Day: 17.2 Earth hours

Year: 84 Earth years

Speed in orbit: 4.2 miles/sec

Average distance from the Sun: 1,783 million miles

Surface temperature: -346°F

Atmosphere: hydrogen, helium, methane

Number of moons: 21

NEPTUNE

LITTLE WAS KNOWN about Neptune since its discovery in 1846 by astronomers John Couch Adams and Urbain Le Verrier, until Voyager 2 paid it a visit in 1989. We now know that Neptune is a featureless globe, streaked by fast-moving clouds and the occasional storm. It also has four extremely faint, dark, icy rings.

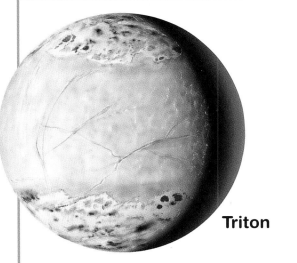

Triton

Neptune's largest moon, Triton, was discovered a few days after the planet itself. It was photographed in great detail by Voyager 2 in 1989. Unlike any other major moon in the Solar System, it orbits in the direction opposite to its parent's rotation. At –391°F it is the coldest place in the Solar System.

Triton's surface is made of a deep layer of granite-hard water and nitrogen ice. It sometimes melts to a slush, then refreezes, producing cracks and ridges. Nitrogen gas builds up beneath the solid ice crust, occasionally bursting out at weak points. These "geysers" spurt gas and black dust up to 5 miles high.

Neptune's internal structure is similar to that of Uranus. Its relatively small rocky core is enclosed in an ocean of warm water containing ammonia and methane gases. Its blueness arises from the small amount of methane in its atmosphere. Winds on Neptune blow at more than 1,200 miles per hour.

Atmosphere

Water, ammonia and methane

Core

NEPTUNE DATAFILE

Diameter: 31,404 miles

Density (water=1): 1.77

Surface gravity (Earth=1): 1.2

Mass (Earth=1) 17.14

Day: 16.1 Earth days

Year: 164.8 Earth years

Speed in orbit: 3.4 miles/sec

Average distance from the Sun: 2,794 million miles

Surface temperature: -364°F

Atmosphere: hydrogen, helium, methane

Number of moons: 11

PLUTO

PLUTO, the smallest, coldest, and outermost planet, was the last to be discovered. It was identified in 1930 by American astronomer Clyde Tombaugh. It was not visited by the Voyager 2, so we still know little about it. Although it has a moon, Charon, Pluto is so small and unusual that some astronomers doubt whether it should be regarded as a planet.

We can only guess what Pluto's surface looks like. It is probably a cratered icescape with Charon large in the sky. The Sun looks like no more than a bright, distant star.

Pluto is quite dense for its size, so it probably has a fairly large, rocky core. This is covered by a mantle of water ice and a crust of nitrogen, carbon monoxide, and methane—frozen hard. The distant Sun provides just enough heat to evaporate surface frost and create a thin atmosphere of nitrogen and methane.

Crust

Mantle

Core

PLUTO DATAFILE

Diameter: 1,444 miles

Density (water=1): 2.1

Surface gravity (Earth=1): 0.04

Mass (Earth=1) 0.002

Day: 6.4 Earth days

Year: 248 Earth years

Speed in orbit: 2.9 miles/sec

Average distance from the Sun: 3,670 million miles

Surface temperature: -364°F

Atmosphere: nitrogen and methane

Number of moons: 1

COMETS

COMETS are lumps of ice and rock, only a few miles across, that orbit the Sun. As they near the Sun, their tails start to grow, eventually extending millions of miles into space. They always point away from the Sun. There is a straight gas tail and a broader, curved dust tail.

Gas tail

Nucleus

Dust tail

A cloud made of billions of icy objects surrounds the Solar System. Called the Oort Cloud, it extends a fifth of the distance to the nearest star. It may be the birthplace of comets. Between the Cloud and the planets, thousands of comet-like objects, which together make up the Kuiper Belt, orbit the sun.

A comet's nucleus is a potato-shaped lump of dust and rock, fused together by frozen gases and water ice. When the comet nears the Sun, the ice melts and the outer crust of the nucleus cracks open. Jets of dust and gas burst out to form a cloud called a coma. Close to the Sun, this cloud is swept back by solar wind, a stream of atomic particles emitted by the Sun, to form two tails.

The nucleus of a comet was first studied in detail when the space probe Giotto flew to within 400 miles of Halley's Comet in 1986. It sent back pictures and sampled the gases and dust particles given off by it.

Sometimes, small fragments break off from comets. Known as meteors or shooting stars, they sometimes approach the Earth in large "showers."

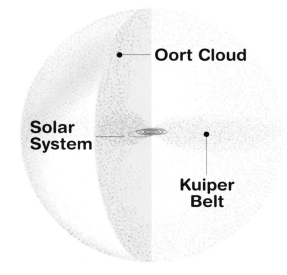

Oort Cloud

Solar System

Kuiper Belt

Dust

Gas

On 30th June 1908, there was an explosion in Earth's atmosphere 4 miles above the Tunguska region of Siberia, Russia. Trees in an area 60 miles across were felled by the blast. It may have been a comet exploding.

OBSERVING SPACE

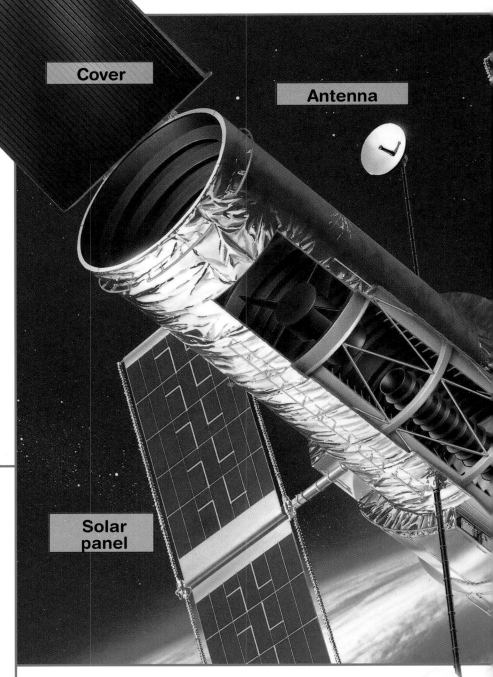

Cover

Antenna

Solar panel

FROM EARTH, we can observe other objects in space: our nearest neighbor, the Moon; our local star, the Sun; the other planets of the Solar System; more distant stars and nebulae, and even other galaxies. Some can be seen with the naked eye, but many more, including objects now known to lie billions of light years away, can only be studied by using powerful telescopes.

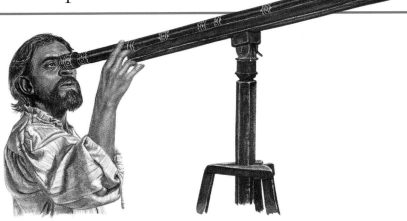

Italian scientist Galileo Galilei was the first person to use a telescope, invented in 1608, to observe space. He discovered mountains and craters on the Moon. Galileo also detected four moons circling Jupiter and witnessed the changing shape of Venus as it orbited the Sun.

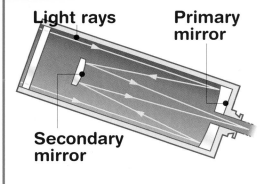

Light rays

Primary mirror

Secondary mirror

There are two kinds of optical telescopes: refractors and reflectors. In a refractor, a convex lens (bulging) collects light from the distant object and focuses it. A reflector uses a concave (dish-shaped) mirror to do the same. Most large modern telescopes are reflectors. In a Cassegrain-type reflector (above), light is focused by two mirrors: a primary and a secondary.

Another type of telescope does not collect light rays at all. Instead, it detects radio waves. Stars and galaxies give off other kinds of radiation as well as light: infrared, ultraviolet, X-rays, and radio waves. There are some objects in space that *only* give off these kinds of radiation. They are otherwise invisible. Large radio telescopes like this one *(left)* look like giant satellite dishes. They are specially designed to collect radio waves and can be turned to face any part of the sky. They are also used in the search for alien life in the Universe.

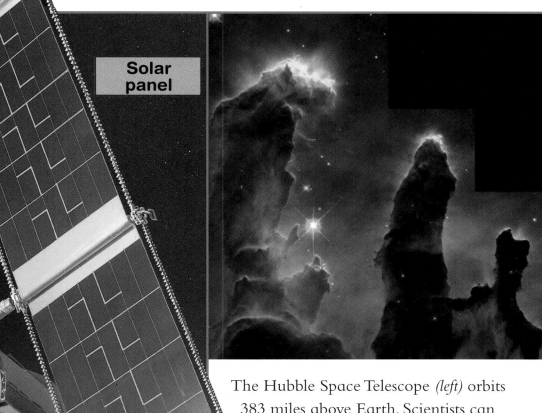

Solar panel

Main mirror

Sensors

The larger the mirror of a reflector, the brighter will be the image of the objects that can be seen through the telescope. The mirror of the world's largest telescope, The Keck *(below)*, located on the summit of Mauna Kea in Hawaii, measures 30 feet across. It consists of 36 hexagon-shaped mirrors fitted together in a honeycomb pattern. The Keck is so sensitive it could detect a candle flickering more than 60,000 miles away.

Modern observatories, where telescopes are housed, are built on mountain tops, above the densest, cloudiest parts of the atmosphere. Mauna Kea, one of the best observing sites in the world, has many observatories.

The Hubble Space Telescope *(left)* orbits 383 miles above Earth. Scientists can point it in any direction and receive pictures of distant stars that are clearer than those taken from most Earth-based telescopes. This is because these telescopes suffer from polluted air, clouds, and atmospheric disturbances. This photograph *(above)*, of stars forming in finger-like columns of gas, was taken by the Hubble, which is so powerful it could detect light from a flashlight 250,000 miles away.

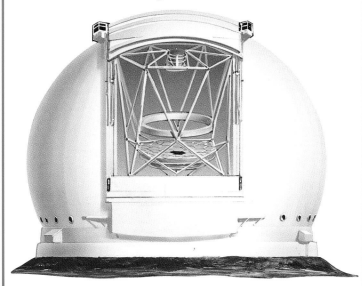

Planet

Milky Way

Comet

Meteors

Moon

A clear, windless night is the best time to observe space from Earth. On many nights, the Moon is the brightest and largest object in the night sky. Up to 3,000 stars may be visible to the naked eye. All of them belong to the Milky Way Galaxy *(see page 4)*. From Earth, our view of one of the Galaxy's spiral arms looks like a misty band across the sky.

This is the "milky way" from which the Galaxy takes its name. Up to five planets (Mercury, Venus, Mars, Jupiter, and Saturn) can also be spotted. You might also catch sight of a comet *(see page 25)*. Shooting stars are streaks of light that last usually for less than a second. They are tiny rock fragments, called meteors, burning up high above Earth.

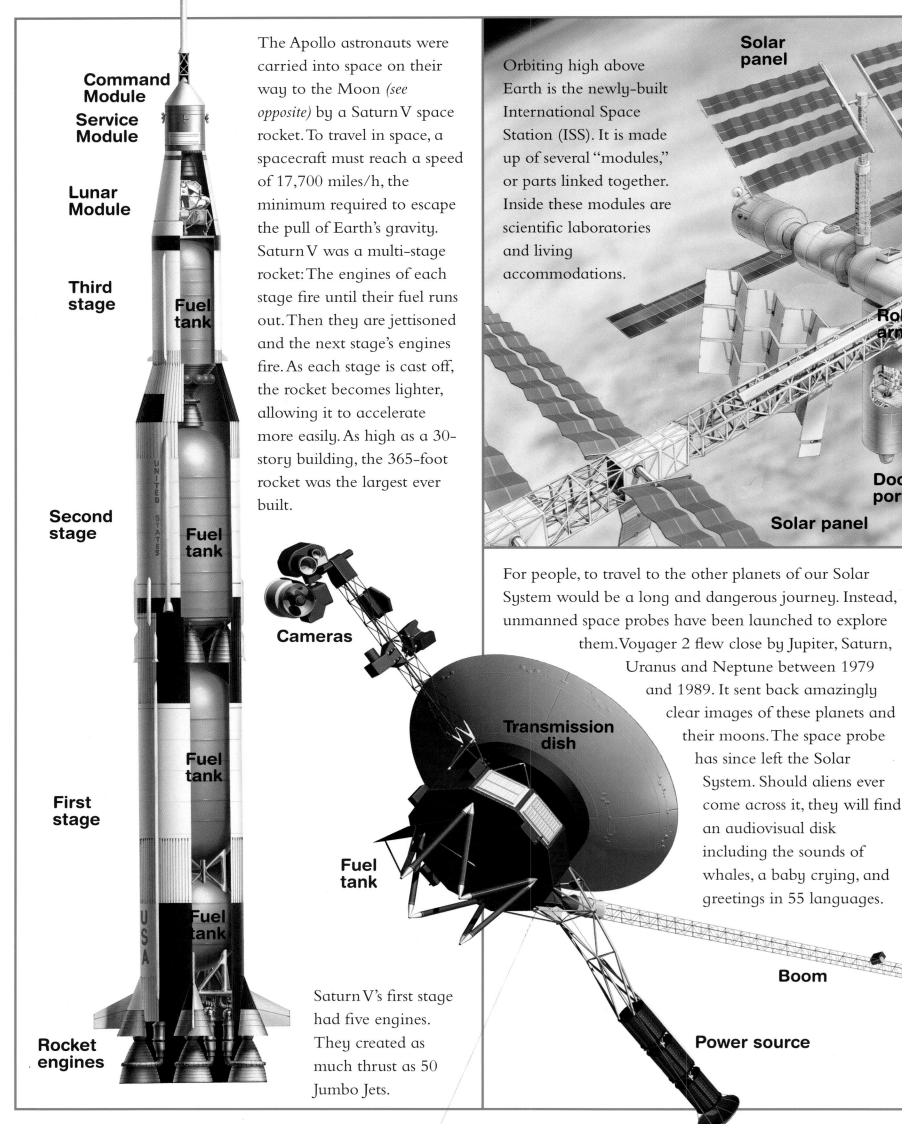

Command Module

Service Module

Lunar Module

Third stage

Fuel tank

Second stage

Fuel tank

First stage

Fuel tank

Fuel tank

Rocket engines

The Apollo astronauts were carried into space on their way to the Moon *(see opposite)* by a Saturn V space rocket. To travel in space, a spacecraft must reach a speed of 17,700 miles/h, the minimum required to escape the pull of Earth's gravity. Saturn V was a multi-stage rocket: The engines of each stage fire until their fuel runs out. Then they are jettisoned and the next stage's engines fire. As each stage is cast off, the rocket becomes lighter, allowing it to accelerate more easily. As high as a 30-story building, the 365-foot rocket was the largest ever built.

Cameras

Saturn V's first stage had five engines. They created as much thrust as 50 Jumbo Jets.

Orbiting high above Earth is the newly-built International Space Station (ISS). It is made up of several "modules," or parts linked together. Inside these modules are scientific laboratories and living accommodations.

Solar panel

Robotic arm

Docking port

Solar panel

For people, to travel to the other planets of our Solar System would be a long and dangerous journey. Instead, unmanned space probes have been launched to explore them. Voyager 2 flew close by Jupiter, Saturn, Uranus and Neptune between 1979 and 1989. It sent back amazingly clear images of these planets and their moons. The space probe has since left the Solar System. Should aliens ever come across it, they will find an audiovisual disk including the sounds of whales, a baby crying, and greetings in 55 languages.

Transmission dish

Fuel tank

Boom

Power source

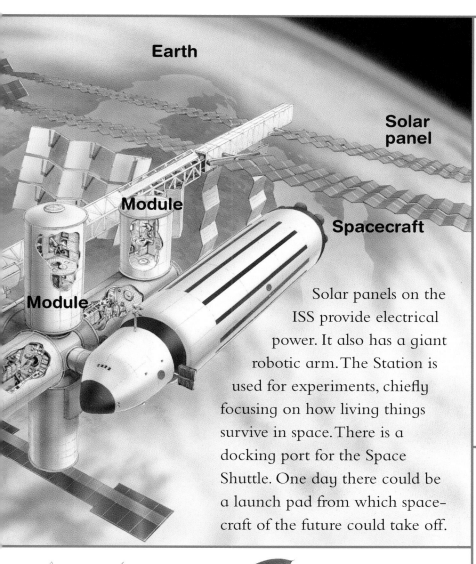

Earth

Solar panel

Module

Spacecraft

Module

Solar panels on the ISS provide electrical power. It also has a giant robotic arm. The Station is used for experiments, chiefly focusing on how living things survive in space. There is a docking port for the Space Shuttle. One day there could be a launch pad from which spacecraft of the future could take off.

SPACE TRAVEL

SPACE begins only about 90 miles above Earth's surface, but it is not easy to get there. Powerful rockets are needed to propel a spacecraft fast enough for it to "escape" Earth's gravity. Once in space, the lack of oxygen, food, and water, plus the dangers of prolonged weightlessness, make any long flight difficult. It may be many years before people travel even to another planet.

The first landing by a manned spacecraft on the Moon took place on July 20th 1969, when the Lunar Module (LM) of Apollo 11 touched down. US astronauts Neil Armstrong and Buzz Aldrin became the first people to step onto the lunar surface. After gathering rock samples and planting a flag, they lifted off in the upper section of the LM to dock with the Command Module (CM) which was orbiting above. There, they rejoined the third astronaut, Michael Collins. The LM was jettisoned (cast off) and the crew returned to Earth in the CM. Five more Apollo missions followed, the last in 1972.

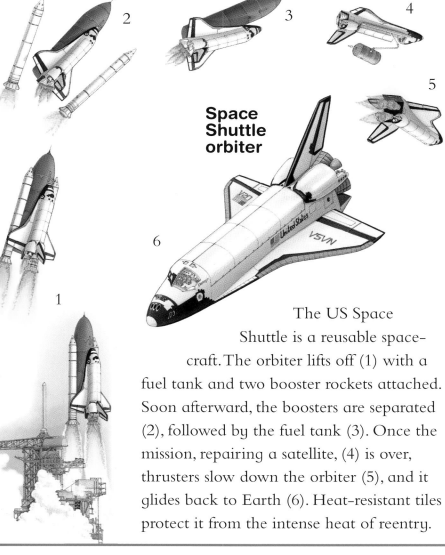

2

3

4

5

Space Shuttle orbiter

6

1

The US Space Shuttle is a reusable spacecraft. The orbiter lifts off (1) with a fuel tank and two booster rockets attached. Soon afterward, the boosters are separated (2), followed by the fuel tank (3). Once the mission, repairing a satellite, (4) is over, thrusters slow down the orbiter (5), and it glides back to Earth (6). Heat-resistant tiles protect it from the intense heat of reentry.

Lunar Module

CONSTELLATIONS

PEOPLE have always been fascinated by the stars of the night sky. Centuries ago, before telescopes were invented, astronomers grouped the stars together in patterns, imagining their shapes to look like gods, people, or animals from popular legends. The ancient Greeks knew of 48 constellations. When Europeans sailed the southern oceans on voyages of exploration, they discovered constellations they had never seen before. Today, the sky is divided into 88 constellations.

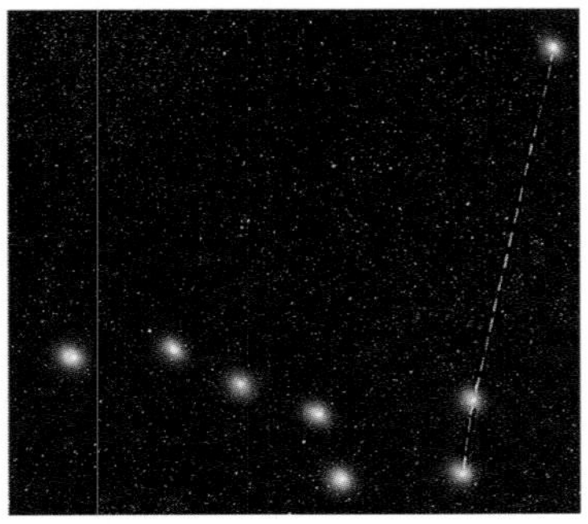

A line running between two stars in the constellation Ursa Major points to the Pole Star, almost exactly due north *(left)*. Constellations also refer to areas of the sky as well as the star patterns they contain. In this way, an interesting star, galaxy, or other object can be given an "address."

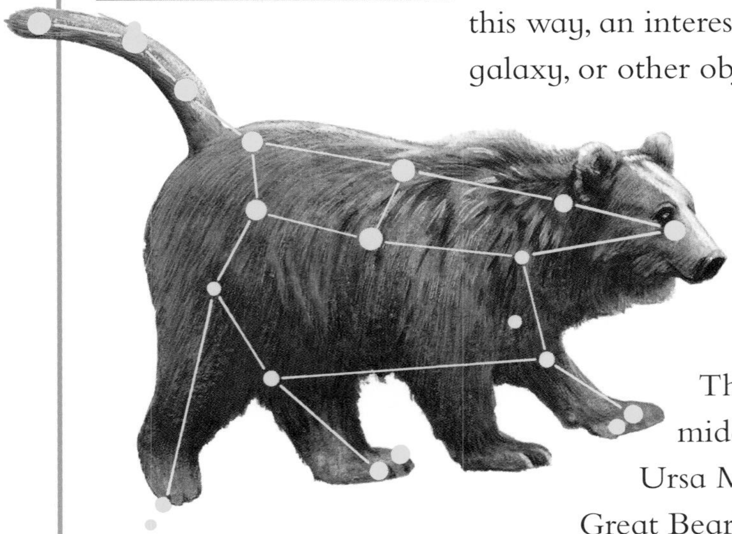

The seven middle stars of Ursa Major (the Great Bear) make up the familiar Plow.

Three stars in a diagonal line form the belt of Orion *(above)*.

A hazy patch of light in Andromeda is a galaxy. It is the most distant object visible to the naked eye.

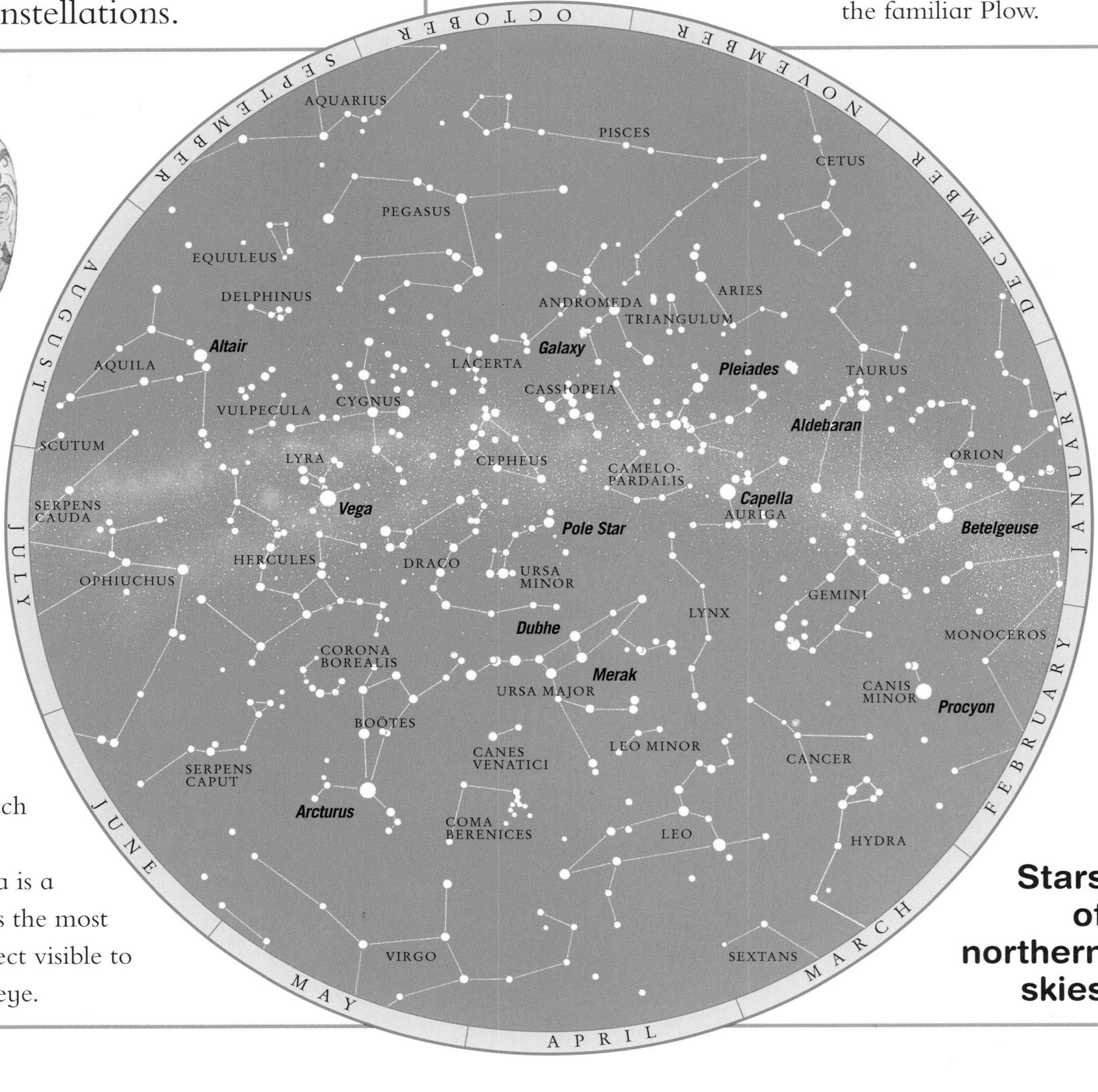

Stars of northern skies

30

Stars of southern skies

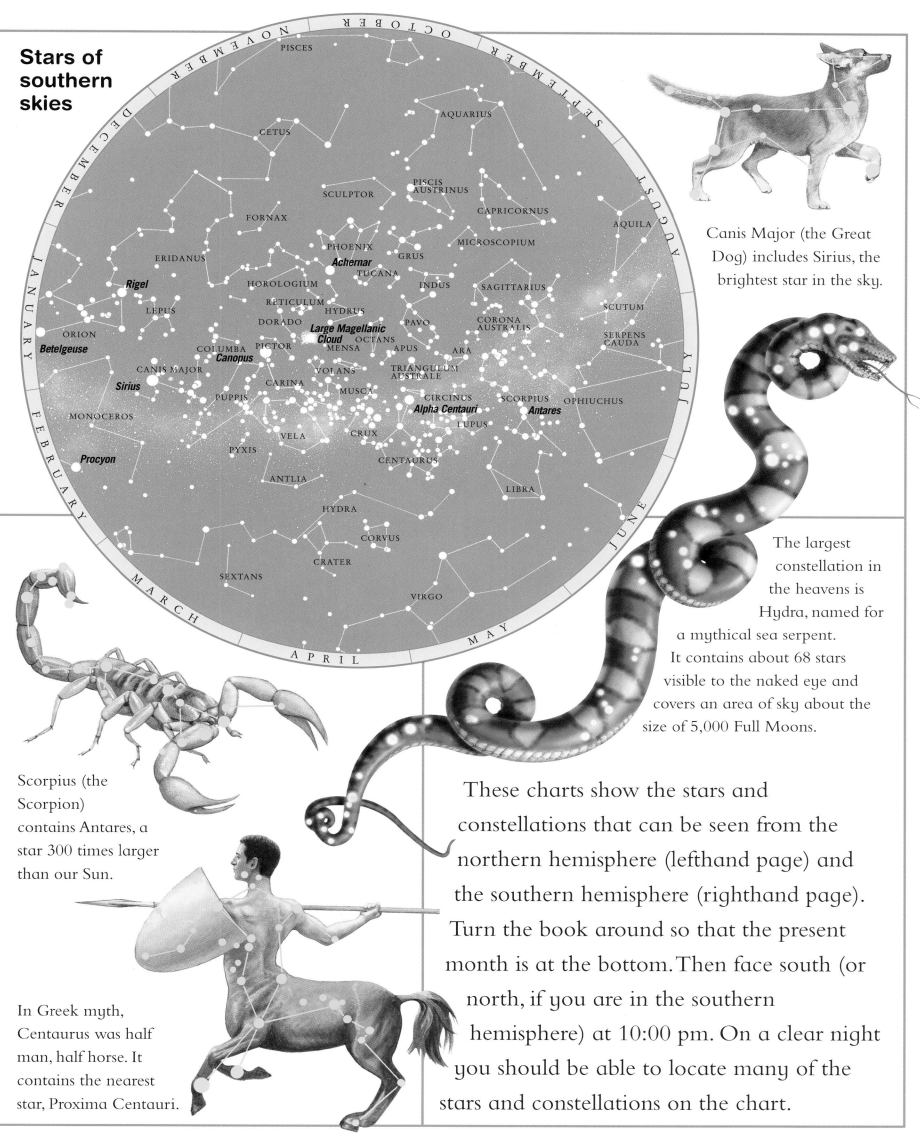

Canis Major (the Great Dog) includes Sirius, the brightest star in the sky.

The largest constellation in the heavens is Hydra, named for a mythical sea serpent. It contains about 68 stars visible to the naked eye and covers an area of sky about the size of 5,000 Full Moons.

Scorpius (the Scorpion) contains Antares, a star 300 times larger than our Sun.

In Greek myth, Centaurus was half man, half horse. It contains the nearest star, Proxima Centauri.

These charts show the stars and constellations that can be seen from the northern hemisphere (lefthand page) and the southern hemisphere (righthand page). Turn the book around so that the present month is at the bottom. Then face south (or north, if you are in the southern hemisphere) at 10:00 pm. On a clear night you should be able to locate many of the stars and constellations on the chart.

INDEX

Photograph acknowledgements:

10 NASA/JPL/Northwestern University; 11 Courtesy of NASA/JPL/Caltech; 12 Jan Curtis; 14 NASA; 15, 21 Courtesy of NASA/JPL/Caltech; 27 Jeff Hester & Paul Scowen (Arizona State University) and NASA